T0132145

Balboa Press books may be ordered through booksellers or by contacting:

Balboa Press
A Division of Hay House
1663 Liberty Drive
Bloomington, IN 47403
www.balboapress.com
1 (877) 407-4847

ISBN: 978-1-9822-3437-9 (sc)
ISBN: 978-1-9822-3438-6 (e)

Print information available on the last page.

Balboa Press rev. date: 09/17/2019

BALBOA
PRESS
A DIVISION OF HAY HOUSE

Joseph's VISIT

Two birdfeeders and a block of suet hang from our front porch where we spent countless hours observing and enjoying a plethora of northeastern birds. Blue jay, grosbeak, woodpecker, cardinal, mourning dove. Chickadee, nuthatch, finch and wren. A symphony of sound and color delighted and charmed us every single day.

In spring, we added hummingbird feeders, often hastily prepared and erected *after* one has appeared at the window next to the porch, or we've been startled by a sudden thrum as a hummer swoops past an ear. When Joseph was alive, he often stood guard, patrolling, protecting this avian food source from the clever, sometimes amusing, but most annoying ……. squirrel.

After work one early spring evening, I sat at the kitchen table before the computer mindlessly deleting a raft of unwanted e-mail when the phone rang. It is my friend, Ellen. We often check in at day's end. As I recall, we were talking about nothing in particular, when from the hallway to my left, in the direction of the bedroom, flies a bird - *in my house!* Over my head it sweeps, landing briefly on the ledge behind the lacey curtain to the right of the round wooden table where I sit.

The sheer curtain, a pattern of trees, rabbits, ducks and birds hangs from a twig about five feet long. The bird seems a bit surprised too at being indoors. It flies around a bit, fluttering its wings furiously against windows. Then somehow it appears to lift straight up vertically and perch atop the hem of the woodland scene veil.

"Joseph! Joseph! It's Joseph!" I exclaim - startled, amazed and very excited. Ellen may have gasped, I don't remember exactly. I do remember her voice - its tone – full and light, energetic but soothing. "Remember to talk softly, calmly and move slowly," she said. My eyes remain fixed on the bird. We hurriedly say our goodbye and promise to reconnect later.

I rush to fling the front door open should it fly in that direction, then retrieve a broom and position its working end so as my visitor can use it to perch upon. "Good, I tell myself. "When he steps on the bristles I will simply slowly and carefully carry the little creature outside." But, no dice. He would not accept my offer. My cat, Mr. Cat, is most interested. He prances about, stretching his inquisitive neck upward toward what might be a hors d'oeuvre or playmate, depending upon his current disposition. I caution him sternly to ditch either thought.

And with an attitude of temporary indulgence, Mr. Cat disappears to the bedroom. I return complete attention to my guest, a white breasted nuthatch. Moving closer, hand on the back of the old oak chair where Joseph usually sat, I whisper, "Joseph? Is that you my love?"

As if in response, it flits from dining to living room, and dives behind the sofa. Uncharacteristically, without a moment's hesitation and seemingly all in one move I follow, bend down and gently pick it up. The bird does not struggle or flail in my cupped hands. It simply nestles into my palm.

I notice no trembling and wonder if perhaps it is dazed.

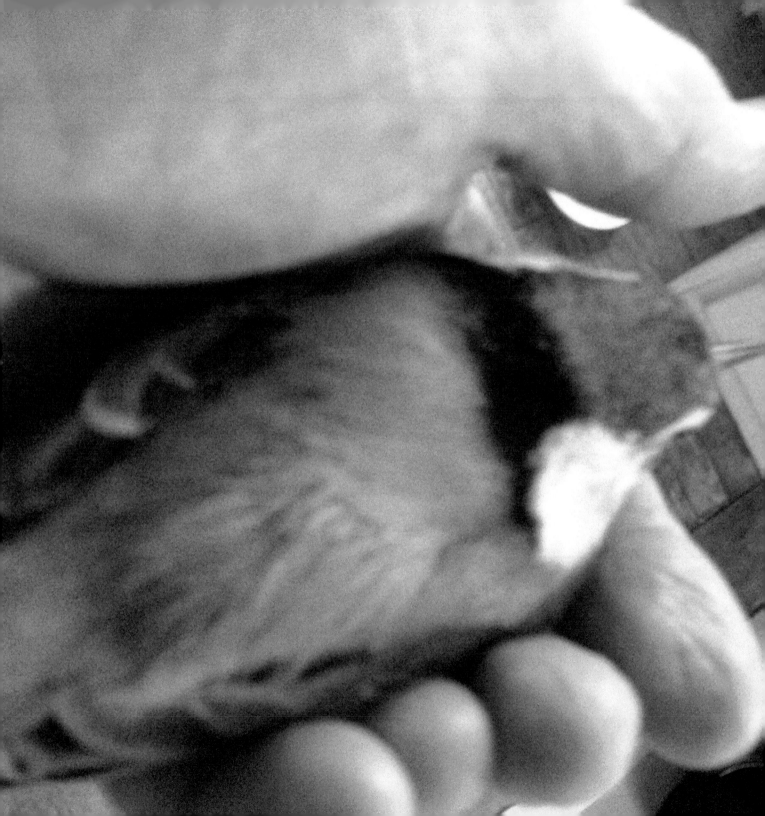

"Joseph, oh Joseph! My darling Joseph. Thank you," I breathe while gently stroking his back. I lift him to my lips and softly kiss the top of his head. "You did it!" And triumphantly set to walking through the house.

Living room, dining room, kitchen. Living room, dining room, kitchen. Hallway, bedroom, bathroom, computer room. Back and forth and around our home. For how long, I do not remember. Mr. Cat reappears accompanying us, his attitude somewhat one of companionship, not predator. Bird rests upon my open hand.

I remember Joseph talking to creatures – chipmunks, ants, wasps, bees, birds, and of course his arch enemy the squirrel. Joseph had great reverence for all living things. However, if he came upon an animal alive but doomed, he'd say, "I don't want to hurt you, " and from a place of great compassion, with reverence, without drama he would swiftly end the suffering with one strong, well placed blow.

Fear rises in me.

"What if you're injured, what am I to do? " I inquire aloud, noticing the quivering in my voice which matches the shakiness in my legs. "I cannot do what you did. Joseph. I just cannot do it. Even if I wanted to, I cannot!" I sob.

It seems we have instantly travelled back in time. It was winter, near the end of his life. I was all worked up at Joseph's determination to walk independently to and from the bathroom those last months. He was so terribly weak, frail and unsteady. With great clarity and resolve he would say, " Please, just let me fall!" And, of course, I couldn't. It was an understandable conundrum we acknowledged, lived with and talked about.

Joseph accepted loving support, care and assistance with grace and dignity. He was not afraid to die, and was always curious if he would remain so when it was officially the end. He commented more than once, when he went into a fall he felt as if he *were* dying.

One instance in particular comes into focus – the one where we both lay on the floor after he had pitched forward and caught me off balance on his way down. Evenly and simply, as a matter of fact, he stated as we lie on the floor face to face, "This is how it's going to happen."

Bird rests in my palm. He looks up blinking, and cocks his head first to one side, then another. As if responding to this as a cue, I stop crying and we step out the back door to the backyard. Smiling, I show him the pond. How the koi fish continue to grow, and the grapes he planted over a decade ago do not. How enjoyable the sound of the waterfall.

I laugh, thank him for the visit and extend my arm upward, encouraging him to perch on a nearby tree branch or simply fly away.

He does not accept my offer. I examine him more closely. He is alert, seems to be able to move or fly and does not appear injured.

"Alright, " I say aloud. "We'll walk some more," so out to the driveway we stroll. It is a bit chilly, this early April evening 36 days since Joseph died. I notice, but do not mind the cold under my stockinged feet or lack of a sweater. My heart is full and warm with wonder. "Look! Look! See how beautiful! How beautiful it is. Our home. Our yard. It's all so lovely. Everything, just as you left it. Isn't it nice?! Comfortable, oh so comfortable. Our oasis.

We cross the yard to the front porch where the feeders and suet hang. I remind this bird in my hand, of how messy he and his species are, how often I must sweep the sunflower shells and what an annoyance it is to have to clean the railings repeatedly, but how really, I don't mind at all and that I will continue to do it as long as I live here. Bird remains attentive, seemingly patient and unconcerned as we round out the tour and reenter the house. We are very much a portrait of how Joseph and I were when he was in his body – so very easy and content in one another's presence, completely absorbed in the present moment however short or long the duration.

I am mindful of time. Nightfall is near.

"You must go," I tell him softly. He does not move, but looks up and does that bird behavior thing with his head.

Food. Maybe some food as I recall seeing stray seeds on the table on the front porch. Back outside we go. I tip him gently from my hand and immediately he eats.

He shakes off unwanted shells from the sunflower seeds and consumes the other round variety whole. "Please," I plead, yet find myself picking him up once again for one more walk through the house.

My disturbance level is rising. What am I to do? It is dusk and dark is soon to come. I return to the table on the porch. I pick him up and kiss his crown, lingering long enough for my mind to take a mental picture and body to note the physical sensations. I deeply inhale this gift of grace I want to remember.

Crying and reluctant, yet with peaceful firm resolve I tip Bird gently back on to the table. I whisper, "I love you," over and over. *Joseph I love you!* I implore him to go. "I can't leave you here. Mr. Cat or some other creature will get you! *Please! Please! Go. Go now, please."*

From deep in me through the depths of all this emotion, erupts one 'thank you' after another. So many tumble up from my heart into my throat in such rhythm, the sound becomes it own song. "Thank you. Thank you. Thank you."

I've no idea how long I stood there chanting this heartfelt appreciation that cries out of me. Not since each of my daughters was placed on my belly after their births have I soared with such joy and humility all at once from such a privileged encounter.

Then, without so much as a flicker of warning my visitor lifts off in the direction of the side yard and in an instant disappears into the darker grey of night's beginning.

There is a lot I do not know about the mystery of death and communicating with the other side. But I do know my very personal experience. Over the years we were together, Joseph and I spoke several times of how he would let me know he was ok after he left his body.

The last conversation we had on the topic was a few weeks before he died during the time of those falls I mentioned earlier. I asked him for a signal if he did indeed find his essence in tact after his physical death. I requested a sign I could not dispute, something that was inarguable. Together we mused about what that might be and eventually came to it having something to do with our beloved birds that come to the feeders on the front porch.

I stand before those feeders now, still feeling the pulsing from the sensation of the nuthatch in my palm. "Spring is here." I look skyward and whisper aloud. "Trees are greening. I'm all right. I'm going to *be* all right. I am ok…….more than ok. "Do not worry, Joseph I miss you to pieces, but I will get through. I will be ok. Thank you! Thank you so much for all that was *and what now is*. See! See the gallery where your art lives and I work.

Remember the sign you made from steel? The black steel letters fairly dance across the building – joseph's gallery. That jaunty red apostrophe brings a smile every time I see it. I love that sign.

It's all beautiful, love. Just beautiful.

Printed in the United States
By Bookmasters